MAK

NORTH AMERICAN
FIELD GUIDES

FRESHWATER FISH

Golriz Golkar

Field Guides

An Imprint of Abdo Reference | abdobooks.com

CONTENTS

WHAT ARE FRESHWATER FISH?

Freshwater fish live part or all of their lives in fresh water. There are more than 10,000 freshwater fish species in the world. They make up nearly half of all fish species. More than 800 freshwater fish species are found in North America. Some species are anadromous. They are born in fresh water. While they live at times in salt water, they always migrate back to fresh water to spawn, or reproduce.

Some freshwater fish swim in large groups called schools, especially when they are young or if they are a small species. This helps them stay safe from predators. A school of fish is usually made up of the same species, swimming in the same direction at the same speed. Other freshwater fish swim alone or in smaller, looser groups.

WHAT ARE FRESHWATER FISH LIKE?

Freshwater fish are cold-blooded vertebrates. Their eyes let them see in two directions at once. Fins help them swim and keep their balance. Gills help them breathe underwater. Most species have fluid-filled channels along their sides, called a lateral line, that allow them to detect water movements. This helps them avoid predators and find prey.

Freshwater fish also lay eggs. Some build egg nests by digging holes in gravel and sand. Some add plant and shell materials to their nests. Others simply lay eggs freely as they swim. Some freshwater fish may live less than five years in the wild. Others live 10 to 15 years. Some very large fish can live up to 100 years.

Some freshwater fish species have adaptations. Special snouts help them smell food. Large eyes help them look for food in muddy waters. Some species, such as catfish, have whisker-like organs called barbels. They help these fish detect prey through smell, taste, and touch. Other fish have specialized fins that help them swim faster.

All fish absorb water through their gills and skin. They must adapt to the salinity of their water habitat, making sure their bodies have just enough salt to survive. Saltwater fish adapt by continuously getting rid of the extra salt their bodies absorb from salt water.

Freshwater fish adapt differently. They drink little water and absorb salt from food and their watery habitat. They store salt in their bodies because they must not lose too much. Then they eliminate extra water through urination to prevent the salt from becoming too diluted.

Water conditions are also critical to freshwater fish species' survival. Some thrive in warm waters, others cold. Some species need clear water, while others need muddy water. Some freshwater fish can handle waters with low oxygen levels. This is typically caused by excess algae that consume oxygen as they die off. Other freshwater fish need specific oxygen amounts to survive.

Close to one-third of all freshwater fish species face environmental threats. These threats may affect an entire species or only those in a specific range. Natural threats include climate change, causing dangers such as unpredictable weather patterns and rising global temperatures. Hybridization, which happens when two different species breed to create a new species, can also reduce the population of a species.

Human-made threats include overfishing, habitat loss from construction and farming, and water pollution. The introduction of invasive species, such as other fish that compete for the same food, can also lead to species decline.

HOW TO USE THIS BOOK

Tab shows the freshwater fish category.

The freshwater fish's common name appears here.

SALMON

PINK SALMON
(ONCORHYNCHUS GORBUSCHA)

Pink salmon are the smallest Pacific salmon species. In the ocean, they have blue-and-green backs, silver sides, and ... Their backs and tail fins have dark spots. In ...ing spawning, males develop dark, humped ...des become red with brown-and-green spots. ...ales develop similar colors. They spawn in

The paragraph gives information about the freshwater fish.

HOW TO SPOT

Size: 20 to 25 inches (50.8 to 63.5 cm) long; 3.5 to 5 pounds (1.6 to 2.3 kg)

Range: Western Canada and northwestern United States

Habitat: Streams, estuaries, and oceans

Diet: Crustaceans, zooplankton, squid, and small fish

OTHER KINDS OF FISH MIGRATION

Catadromous fish are born in salty ocean water, live most of their lives in fresh water, and return to salt water to spawn. Eels are catadromous, and the American eel is the only freshwater eel species found in North America. Amphidromous fish move between fresh water and salt ... entire lives, but not to spawn.

Sidebars provide additional information about the topic.

14

The freshwater fish's scientific name appears here.

SOCKEYE SALMON
(ONCORHYNCHUS NERKA)

In the ocean, sockeye salmon have silver sides, white bellies, and green-and-blue upper bodies. In fresh water during spawning, their heads turn green and their bodies turn bright red. Nonmigratory sockeye subspecies called kokanee have blue backs and silver sides. Kokanee salmon always live in fresh water. Spawning males develop humped backs and hooked jaws with tiny teeth. They spawn in summer or fall. Sockeye salmon get their bright colors from the zooplankton they eat.

HOW TO SPOT

Size: 18 to 30 inches (45.7 to 76.2 cm) long; 4 to 15 pounds (1.8 to 6.8 kg)
Range: Northwestern and western United States
Habitat: Lakes, streams, rivers, estuaries, and oceans
Diet: Zooplankton, crustaceans, and small fish

How to Spot features give information about the freshwater fish's size, range, habitat, and diet.

Fun Facts give interesting information about freshwater fish.

FUN FACT

Migrating salmon use their sense of smell to identify their home stream when returning to fresh water for spawning.

Images show the freshwater fish.

15

ARCTIC GRAYLING
(THYMALLUS ARCTICUS)

Arctic graylings, members of the salmon family, have a large dorsal fin and scalloped edges. They have dark backs and black, silver, gold, or blue sides. Their heads have black spots, and their dorsal fins have shiny spots that are red, blue, or purple. Some arctic graylings migrate between streams and lakes. Others stay in the same area their entire lives. They spawn in spring and summer. In winter, they eat little and save energy by living in slow-moving waters. They can handle low oxygen levels, allowing them to survive long winters in places where many fish cannot live.

HOW TO SPOT

Size: 10 to 12 inches (25.4 to 30.5 cm) long; 5.1 pounds (2.3 kg)

Range: Northeastern Canada; Alaska and northwestern United States

Habitat: Streams and lakes

Diet: Insects, fish eggs, and small fish

WHAT ARE SALMON?

Salmon are long, slender fish of the Salmonidae family. North American species include seven Pacific species and one Atlantic species. Most species of this anadromous fish are born in fresh water and migrate to the ocean. To spawn, they migrate back to their birthplace. All Pacific species die after spawning.

ATLANTIC SALMON *(SALMO SALAR)*

Atlantic salmon change colors many times. In fresh water as young fish, they are bronze with dark vertical bars. Red-and-black spots camouflage them from predators. In the ocean as adults, they develop silver sides, black backs, and white bellies. In fresh water during spawning, they turn silver and bronze. Atlantic salmon migrate long distances from rivers to the Atlantic Ocean. They spend between one and three years in salt water before spawning in fresh water. Pollution, overfishing, and construction have reduced their population. They are protected and cannot be fished in North America.

HOW TO SPOT

Size: 28 to 30 inches (71.1 to 76.2 cm) long; 8 to 12 pounds (3.6 to 5.4 kg)

Range: Canada and eastern United States

Habitat: Rivers and oceans

Diet: Insects, crustaceans, zooplankton, and fish

FUN FACT
Some Atlantic salmon die after spawning, and others may survive long enough to spawn several times in their lives.

9

CHINOOK SALMON
(ONCORHYNCHUS TSHAWYTSCHA)

In an ocean habitat, chinook salmon have blue-and-green backs and heads. Their sides are silver, and their bellies are white. Black spots cover their upper bodies and tail fins. In fresh water during spawning, they turn olive green, red, or purple. Spawning males develop hooked upper jaws. They spend a few years feeding in the ocean before returning to fresh water to spawn in summer or fall.

HOW TO SPOT

Size: 3 to 4.9 feet (0.9 to 1.5 m) long; 30 to 130 pounds (13.6 to 60 kg)

Range: Alaska and West Coast of United States, western and northwestern Canada

Habitat: Streams, rivers, estuaries, and oceans

Diet: Crustaceans, insects, and fish

FUN FACT

Chinook salmon are the largest species of Pacific salmon. Because of their size, they are also called king salmon.

CHUM SALMON *(ONCORHYNCHUS KETA)*

Chum salmon are among the largest salmon species. In an ocean habitat, they are metallic green and blue with black speckles. In fresh water, they have red-and-black stripes. Young chum salmon have vertical bars and spots that disappear once they are in the ocean. Spawning males develop large teeth and mottled bodies with red-and-black lines. They spawn from summer to the following spring. Young chum salmon often eat insects. Adults also eat fish, snails, and squid.

HOW TO SPOT

Size: 24 to 28 inches (61 to 71.1 cm) long; 10 to 35 pounds (4.5 to 15.9 kg)

Range: Northern Canada and western United States

Habitat: Streams, rivers, estuaries, and oceans

Diet: Insects, fish, and squid

COHO SALMON
(ONCORHYNCHUS KISUTCH)

In the ocean, coho salmon have dark metallic-blue or green backs and lighter bellies. Their sides are silver, and their backs and upper tails are spotted with black. In fresh water during spawning, their sides become red and their bodies darken. Spawning males develop hooked snouts and large teeth. Coho salmon spawn in fall or winter. Some migrate more than 1,000 miles (1,609.3 km) to reach the ocean. Others migrate short distances to ocean waters close to their freshwater birthplace.

HOW TO SPOT

Size: 24 to 30 inches (61 to 76.2 cm) long; 8 to 35 pounds (3.6 to 15.9 kg)

Range: Alaska and West Coast of United States and western and northwestern Canada

Habitat: Streams, rivers, estuaries, and oceans

Diet: Zooplankton, crustaceans, insects, and small fish

LAKE WHITEFISH
(COREGONUS CLUPEAFORMIS)

Lake whitefish have small heads and blunt snouts. They have silver bodies with green-and-brown backs. These fish are native to the Great Lakes of the United States. When they spawn in the fall, adults swim to shallow water. They spawn over rocky shoals where ice protects the eggs from storms. Lake whitefish are cold-water fish. When water becomes too warm, they collect in schools and swim to colder depths. As climate change raises Earth's average temperature, these fish may lose the cold-water habitat they need to survive.

FUN FACT
People have eaten lake whitefish for thousands of years. Native Americans have used the fish to make a powder for stews and pies.

HOW TO SPOT

Size: 17 to 22 inches (43.2 to 55.9 cm) long; 1.5 to 4 pounds (0.7 to 1.8 kg)

Range: Canada and the Great Lakes

Habitat: Lakes

Diet: Zooplankton, small fish, and fish eggs

PINK SALMON
(ONCORHYNCHUS GORBUSCHA)

Pink salmon are the smallest Pacific salmon species. In the ocean, they have blue-and-green backs, silver sides, and white bellies. Their backs and tail fins have dark spots. In fresh water during spawning, males develop dark, humped backs. Their sides become red with brown-and-green spots. Spawning females develop similar colors. They spawn in summer or fall.

HOW TO SPOT

Size: 20 to 25 inches (50.8 to 63.5 cm) long; 3.5 to 5 pounds (1.6 to 2.3 kg)

Range: Western Canada and northwestern United States

Habitat: Streams, estuaries, and oceans

Diet: Crustaceans, zooplankton, squid, and small fish

OTHER KINDS OF FISH MIGRATION

Catadromous fish are born in salty ocean water, live most of their lives in fresh water, and return to salt water to spawn. Eels are catadromous, and the American eel is the only freshwater eel species found in North America. Amphidromous fish move between fresh water and salt water their entire lives, but not to spawn.

SOCKEYE SALMON
(ONCORHYNCHUS NERKA)

In the ocean, sockeye salmon have silver sides, white bellies, and green-and-blue upper bodies. In fresh water during spawning, their heads turn green and their bodies turn bright red. Nonmigratory sockeye subspecies called kokanee have blue backs and silver sides. Kokanee salmon always live in fresh water. Spawning males develop humped backs and hooked jaws with tiny teeth. They spawn in summer or fall. Sockeye salmon get their bright colors from the zooplankton they eat.

HOW TO SPOT

Size: 18 to 30 inches (45.7 to 76.2 cm) long; 4 to 15 pounds (1.8 to 6.8 kg)

Range: Northwestern and western United States

Habitat: Lakes, streams, rivers, estuaries, and oceans

Diet: Zooplankton, crustaceans, and small fish

FUN FACT
Migrating salmon use their sense of smell to identify their home stream when returning to fresh water for spawning.

APACHE TROUT
(ONCORHYNCHUS APACHE)

Apache trout have yellow-and-gold bodies with olive-green heads and backs. A yellow-orange stripe crosses their throats. Large, dark spots cover their bodies. They are found only in Arizona's White Mountains. Young fish live in shallow waters, while adults lurk in deeper waters. They spawn in spring. Other trout compete with this species for food and eat their young. They are a protected species. They were first protected in the 1950s by the White Mountain Apache Tribe, who banned trout fishing on their land.

HOW TO SPOT

Size: 5.1 to 9.1 inches (13 to 23.1 cm) long; 0.4 to 6 pounds (0.2 to 2.7 kg)

Range: Arizona in the United States

Habitat: Streams, rivers, and lakes

Diet: Insects, leeches, fish, and crustaceans

WHAT ARE TROUT AND CHAR?

Trout and char belong to the Salmonidae family. They are long and slender. Most trout belong to two subfamilies: Oncorhynchus and Salvelinus. These two subfamilies differ in body coloring, bone shape in the mouth, and teeth placement. Char have unique teeth placement, and they have lighter spots and smaller scales than salmon and trout.

BROOK TROUT *(SALVELINUS FONTINALIS)*

Brook trout are a type of char. They have yellow-spotted, green backs. Their sides are orange or red with reddish spots. Their lower fins are orange or red, each with a black and a white streak. Their bellies are white. During the fall spawning season, their colors deepen. Spawning males develop orange-and-red sides and black-striped bellies. Brook trout live in clean, cool mountain streams. They spend their days in deep, cold waters and swim to the surface at night.

HOW TO SPOT

Size: 9 to 10 inches (22.9 to 25.4 cm) long; 1 to 5 pounds (0.5 to 2.3 kg)

Range: Canada and northeastern and central United States

Habitat: Streams, ponds, and lakes

Diet: Phytoplankton, invertebrates, and insects

BULL TROUT *(SALVELINUS CONFLUENTUS)*

Bull trout are olive-green char with orange spots on their sides. Some spend their entire lives in the same stream. Anadromous species migrate to oceans and return to fresh water for spawning between summer and fall. They live mostly in cold mountain and coastal streams. During spawning migration, they swim to smaller streams. Young bull trout eat insects, while adults eat fish. Threats to their survival include habitat loss, dam construction that blocks migration, and competition or predation from non-native species.

HOW TO SPOT

Size: 25 to 40.5 inches (63.5 to 102.9 cm) long; 31 pounds (14.1 kg)

Range: Canada and northwestern United States

Habitat: Streams, rivers, lakes, and oceans

Diet: Insects and fish

FUN FACT

Bull trout sometimes breed with brook trout. Their young, however, cannot have babies, leading to decreased populations of both species.

CALIFORNIA GOLDEN TROUT
(ONCORHYNCHUS AGUABONITA)

California golden trout have yellow-gold bodies. Their sides have red bands and big, dark spots. Their bellies are deep red. Their fins and tails have small, black spots. These trout are native to the South Fork Kern River in California and its tributaries. They have also been raised in hatcheries and released in other states. California golden trout live in cold, clear streams. Spawning occurs in summer. A lack of predators makes them more active in the daytime than other trout. Hybridization with rainbow trout is reducing their population.

HOW TO SPOT

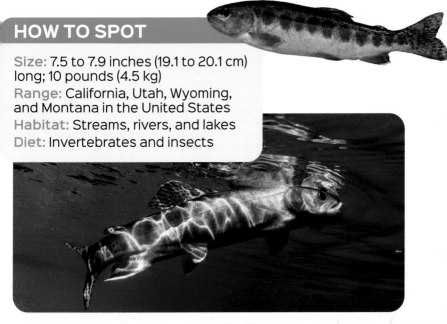

Size: 7.5 to 7.9 inches (19.1 to 20.1 cm) long; 10 pounds (4.5 kg)
Range: California, Utah, Wyoming, and Montana in the United States
Habitat: Streams, rivers, and lakes
Diet: Invertebrates and insects

FISH HYBRIDIZATION

Many freshwater fish hybridize in the wild. This likely happens so that the best traits of two species are passed on, increasing the new species' chance of survival. But hybridization causes problems too. Populations of threatened fish species decline as fewer fish are born and food competition with other fish species increases.

CUTTHROAT TROUT
(ONCORHYNCHUS CLARKII)

Cutthroat trout have green, brown, or golden bodies with red, pink, or orange gills. Their backs, sides, and fins are spotted. They are native to the cold-water tributaries of the Pacific Ocean, Rocky Mountain, and Great Basin regions. Some are anadromous. They spawn in the spring. There are more than 14 subspecies of cutthroat trout, which often compete with other trout species for the same food. Habitat loss, sport fishing, and hybridization—or breeding with other species—have led to their decline.

HOW TO SPOT

Size: 6 to 22 inches (15.2 to 55.9 cm) long; 4.4 to 8.8 pounds (2 to 4 kg)

Range: Southern Canada and western United States

Habitat: Lakes, rivers, streams, and saltwater tributaries

Diet: Insects, small fish, frogs, fish eggs, and plants

FUN FACT

Cutthroat trout get their name from the bright-red streaks beneath their lower jaws.

DOLLY VARDEN *(SALVELINUS MALMA)*

Dolly Varden are colorful char. Some forms are anadromous. In the ocean, adults are silver and green with orange spots. Once they reach fresh water, they turn greenish brown with red-orange spots. Full-time freshwater Dolly Varden are smaller and have green-brown or silver-gray sides with red-orange spots. Spawning males and females develop red, black, and white bellies, red-orange spots, and dark fins. Some freshwater Dolly Varden live in a single stream their entire lives. Young Dolly Varden eat insects and larvae. Adults eat fish and scavenge for salmon eggs.

HOW TO SPOT

Size: 12 to 30 inches (30.5 to 76.2 cm) long; 10 to 27 pounds (4.5 to 12.2 kg)
Range: Northern Canada and northwestern United States
Habitat: Streams, lakes, estuaries, and oceans
Diet: Insects, larvae, crustaceans, salmon eggs, and small fish

GILA TROUT *(ONCORHYNCHUS GILAE)*

Gila trout are among the least common trout species in the United States. They have yellow-and-brown upper bodies. Their golden sides and bellies have black spots, and a pink stripe runs across each side. Gila trout once lived in a wide range, but climate and landscape changes restricted their movement. They now live in small streams, and they are smaller in size because they have little space to grow. Spawning occurs in spring when waters warm. Their population is declining due to wildfire air pollution, food competition, and hybridization with species such as rainbow trout.

HOW TO SPOT

Size: 5.1 to 9.1 inches (13 to 23.1 cm) long; 1 to 6 ounces (28 to 170 g)

Range: New Mexico and Arizona in the United States

Habitat: Streams

Diet: Insects

LAKE TROUT *(SALVELINUS NAMAYCUSH)*

Despite their name, lake trout are a type of char. They have forked tails, dark backs, and white bellies. Light spots cover their gray sides. Their lower fins are orange. Lake trout live in very cold water. They are found at river bottoms and lake depths of 50 feet (15.2 m) or more. Spawning occurs in the fall. Most lake trout are top predators that feed on other fish in the Great Lakes. They keep the food web balanced. Young fish eat phytoplankton, invertebrates, and insects. Adults eat mainly fish.

HOW TO SPOT

Size: 36 inches (91.4 cm) long; 40 pounds (18.1 kg)

Range: Eastern Canada, Great Lakes, and northwestern United States

Habitat: Lakes, rivers, and streams

Diet: Phytoplankton, invertebrates, insects, and fish

FUN FACT
During spawning season, males and females may spawn in groups with other lake trout.

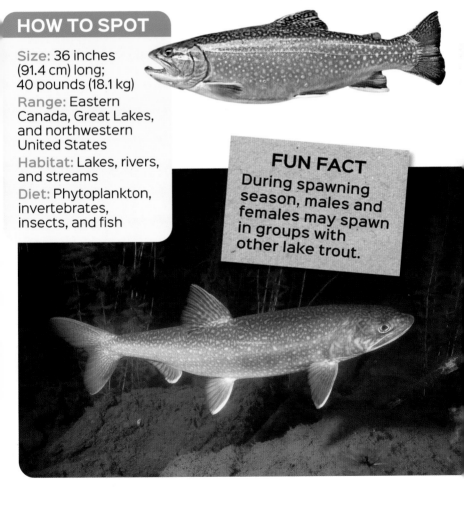

RAINBOW TROUT
(ONCORHYNCHUS MYKISS)

Rainbow trout are blue green or yellow green with pink streaks. Their bellies are white. Their backs and fins have black spots. Rainbow trout mostly live in freshwater habitats. Migratory rainbow trout—called steelheads—spend time in the ocean. They return to streams to spawn, often in the spring. The young of two steelheads may become a freshwater rainbow trout. The young of two freshwater rainbow trout may become a steelhead. Rainbow trout may hybridize with brown trout, gila trout, and golden trout.

FUN FACT

Steelheads can jump 11 feet (3.4 m) in the air when climbing waterfalls. They can also speed up from 0 to 25 miles per hour (40.2 kmh) in a second.

HOW TO SPOT

Size: 20 to 30 inches (50.8 to 76.2 cm) long; 8 pounds (3.6 kg)

Range: Western and central United States

Habitat: Rivers, streams, and lakes

Diet: Insects, small fish, and crustaceans

REDBAND TROUT
(ONCORHYNCHUS MYKISS GAIRDNERI)

Redband trout are a subspecies of rainbow trout. One population lives in the Columbia River and the other in the Great Basin. They have silvery-brown bodies with small, black spots and red bands on their sides, giving the fish its name. River-dwellers have an orange mark under their throats, a red stripe across their chests, and yellow or orange bellies. These trout spawn anytime from winter to summer. Threats include habitat loss, invasive species, and climate change. For these reasons, their habitats are highly protected.

HOW TO SPOT

Size: 10 to 30 inches (25.4 to 76.2 cm) long; 1 to 3 pounds (0.5 to 1.4 kg)
Range: Western United States
Habitat: Streams, rivers, and lakes
Diet: Invertebrates and insects

FUN FACT
Redband trout are well-adapted to desert climates. They can handle higher water temperatures and lower oxygen levels than most rainbow trout.

LAKE STURGEON
(ACIPENSER FULVESCENS)

Lake sturgeon are long and slender with wide snouts. Their bodies are green and gray with dark, scattered spots. These purely freshwater fish migrate to lakeshores in the summer to spawn. Spawning begins at about age 15 for males and 24 for females and occurs every four to six years. Males may live to about 50 years old, while females have lived as long as 150 years. Lake sturgeon are the oldest and largest native species of the Great Lakes. Their population has decreased because of overfishing, pollution, and an inability to spawn because of dam construction.

HOW TO SPOT

Size: 6.6 feet (2 m) long; 200 pounds (90.7 kg)
Range: Canada and central United States
Habitat: Rivers and lakes
Diet: Crayfish, snails, clams, and leeches

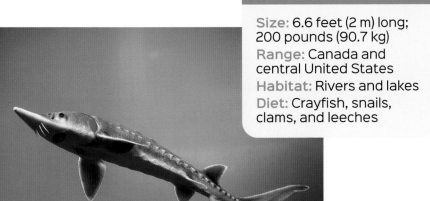

WHAT ARE STURGEON?

Sturgeon are a family of 29 large, long-living fish species. Eight species live in North America. Some are anadromous, and others are purely freshwater fish. Instead of scales, bony plates called scutes cover a sturgeon's body. These bottom-dwellers have barbels to detect prey and large mouths to suck them up.

WHITE STURGEON
(ACIPENSER TRANSMONTANUS)

White sturgeon are the largest freshwater fish in North America. These sturgeon have wide snouts, white bellies, and light-gray backs. They rely on water temperature, daylight, and water current speed to know when to spawn. While they are anadromous, some live in fresh water their entire lives if they cannot reach the ocean. Otherwise, they migrate to the ocean during nonspawning periods. Young white sturgeon eat small invertebrates and mollusks along river bottoms. Adults eat mostly fish.

HOW TO SPOT

Size: 12.5 to 20 feet (3.8 to 6 m) long; 990 to 1,500 pounds (449.1 to 680.4 kg)

Range: Western Canada and western United States

Habitat: Streams, rivers, estuaries, and oceans

Diet: Clams, mussels, worms, fish eggs, and fish

FUN FACT
White sturgeon have the unusual quality of growing their whole lives. They can also live much longer than most freshwater fish—past 100 years old.

BANDED SUNFISH
(ENNEACANTHUS OBESUS)

Banded sunfish have small, round bodies and rounded tail fins. They live in slow-moving waters filled with aquatic plants. They have brown backs, lighter-brown sides, and tan bellies. Vertical stripes run down their sides. Yellow spots cover their bodies and fins. Males turn dark with bright spots during spring and summer spawning. Banded sunfish live in acidic and shallow waters. They survive only in protected backwater areas because they are prey for large fish.

HOW TO SPOT

Size: 1 to 3 inches (2.5 to 7.6 cm) long; weight unknown
Range: Eastern United States
Habitat: Ponds, streams, and swamps
Diet: Insects and crustaceans

WHAT ARE SUNFISH?

Sunfish are a family of about 30 North American freshwater fish species. They vary in size, have narrow bodies when looked at head-on, and have a single dorsal fin with a spiny part and a soft part. Sunfish build nests in shallow waters by using their tails to make a pit in gravel, mud, or stone bottom surfaces.

BLACK CRAPPIE
(POMOXIS NIGROMACULATUS)

Black crappie are larger than white crappie. Their bodies are silver and green. They have irregular patterns of speckles and blotches instead of stripes. Black crappie can be found in 48 states. They live in quiet, warm waters, often hiding under plants, rocks, and fallen trees. They spawn in the spring. These sunfish are also host fish for mussels. The mussels attach to the fish's gills for a few weeks after birth to continue growing. Black crappie often compete with walleye for food, such as small fish and crustaceans.

HOW TO SPOT

Size: 10.8 to 19.3 inches (27.4 to 49 cm) long; 6 pounds (2.7 kg)

Range: United States and southern Canada

Habitat: Lakes, ponds, and streams

Diet: Larvae, crustaceans, and small fish

BLUEGILL *(LEPOMIS MACROCHIRUS)*

Bluegill are small, round fish with small mouths. They have dark-brown or olive-green backs and green or blue-brown sides with yellow bellies. A blue flap near their gills gives the fish its name. Spawning males develop orange-red chests and blue jaws. Bluegill are native to the central and southern United States but are found all over the country. They often search for prey and hide from predators in weed beds, choosing lakes and slow-moving streams as their home. They spawn in the spring and may breed with other sunfish species.

HOW TO SPOT

Size: 6 to 9 inches (15.2 to 22.9 cm) long; 8 ounces (226.8 g)
Range: United States
Habitat: Lakes, rivers, ponds, and streams
Diet: Insects, snails, zooplankton, fish eggs, and fish

GREEN SUNFISH *(LEPOMIS CYANELLUS)*

Green sunfish are large sunfish with large mouths. Their upper bodies are dark green. Their sides are light green with vertical stripes. Their bellies are yellow or white, and light-green spots cover their bodies. Green sunfish adjust easily to a changing environment. They can overpopulate small lakes or ponds. They are native to the region west of the Appalachian Mountains and east of the Rocky Mountains. Spawning occurs in the spring and summer. They often hybridize with other sunfish species.

HOW TO SPOT

Size: 3 to 6 inches (7.6 to 15.2 cm) long; 8 to 12.8 ounces (226.8 to 362.9 g)

Range: United States and northeastern Mexico

Habitat: Streams, rivers, ponds, and tributaries

Diet: Insects, small fish, and larvae

GUADALUPE BASS
(MICROPTERUS TRECULII)

Guadalupe bass have long, slender bodies and upturned mouths. Their bodies are olive green, and their bellies are white. Dark horizontal stripes run across their backs. Their coloring remains the same when they spawn in the spring or summer. Guadalupe bass are found only in the streams of the Edwards Plateau in Texas. Young fish eat insects and larvae, while adults eat mostly crayfish and fish. To keep the small population safe, Texas laws require that these fish be released when caught.

HOW TO SPOT

Size: 12 to 18 inches (30.5 to 45.7 cm) long; 1 pound (0.5 kg)
Range: Texas in the United States
Habitat: Streams and reservoirs
Diet: Insects, larvae, crayfish, and fish

FUN FACT
After females lay their eggs, males chase the females away and protect the eggs on their own.

LARGEMOUTH BASS
(MICROPTERUS SALMOIDES)

Largemouth bass have especially large mouths for a sunfish. They have olive-green backs and sides. Their bellies are beige, and young fish have reddish tails with a dark vertical band. They are native to the eastern United States but are stocked throughout North America. Largemouth bass adapt well to many freshwater habitats but live mostly in clear, still water. Spawning occurs in the spring when waters warm. They are top predators in most habitats. Adults eat mostly other fish, hiding among plants before attacking prey.

HOW TO SPOT

Size: 6 to 18 inches (15.2 to 45.7 cm) long; 1 to 20 pounds (0.5 to 9.1 kg)

Range: United States, Mexico, and southern Canada

Habitat: Lakes, ponds, streams, and rivers

Diet: Zooplankton, larvae, fish, and invertebrates

LONGEAR SUNFISH
(LEPOMIS MEGALOTIS)

Longear sunfish are small and round with medium-sized mouths. Their heads are olive green or orange with blue markings. Their blue-green backs and sides are speckled with yellow and green. Their bellies are yellow or orange. Their gill flap looks like a long ear, giving this sunfish its name. They are found mostly in the Mississippi River and Great Lakes regions in clear waters with aquatic plants. They visit shallow, warm water during spring or summer spawning. Longear sunfish are better than other sunfish at grabbing food in fast-moving waters.

HOW TO SPOT

Size: 5 to 6 inches (12.7 to 15.2 cm) long; 1 pound (0.5 kg)

Range: United States, southern Canada, and northern Mexico

Habitat: Lakes, streams, and rivers

Diet: Insects, crustaceans, fish eggs, and fish

FUN FACT

Longear sunfish often gather around nests of other sunfish, including their own species, ready to grab the eggs for a meal.

OZARK BASS
(AMBLOPLITES CONSTELLATUS)

Ozark bass are slender sunfish with brown-and-green bodies. Small, dark speckles surround their big, red eyes. They are found only in the White River drainage area of Arkansas and Missouri. Ozark bass need clear, cold water. They often swim in shady areas of rocky pools, creeks, and rivers with boulders and brush nearby. Spawning season begins in the spring when waters warm. Rather than the females, Ozark bass males build and guard nests. Their population is threatened by habitat loss, lack of food, water pollution, and climate change.

HOW TO SPOT

Size: 7.5 inches (19.1 cm) long; 1 pound (0.5 kg)
Range: Arkansas, Missouri, and Oklahoma in the United States
Habitat: Streams, rivers, and creeks
Diet: Insects, minnows, and crayfish

PUMPKINSEED SUNFISH
(LEPOMIS GIBBOSUS)

Pumpkinseed sunfish have a pumpkin-seed shape and a slightly forked tail. They have olive-green backs, yellow or orange bellies, and yellow sides spotted with red, orange, and blue. Their cheeks and gills have blue, green, and yellow bands. Eight vertical stripes run across their sides. These sunfish live in warm, shallow, and clear waters. They lurk among aquatic plants, hiding from predators such as largemouth bass, pike perch, and herons. Spawning occurs in the spring or summer.

HOW TO SPOT

Size: 3 to 8 inches (7.6 to 20.3 cm) long; 1 pound (0.5 kg)

Range: Southeastern Canada and central and southern United States

Habitat: Lakes, ponds, and rivers

Diet: Insects, larvae, snails, crustaceans, and worms

FUN FACT
Female pumpkinseed sunfish often lay eggs in several nests, so a nest may hold eggs from different mothers.

REDBREAST SUNFISH
(LEPOMIS AURITUS)

Redbreast sunfish are large, flat sunfish. Their upper bodies are blue and green. Females have orange and yellow bellies. Males have orange-and-red bellies. Their fins are red tipped. Both males and females have vertical rows of reddish-brown spots on their sides. These sunfish live in clear, slow-moving waters with tree stumps or woody debris but no plants. They spawn in the spring or summer in shallow waters. Redbreast sunfish often hybridize with other sunfish species.

HOW TO SPOT

Size: 2 to 9 inches (5.1 to 22.9 cm) long; 3.2 to 6.4 ounces (90.7 to 181.4 g)

Range: Southeastern Canada and eastern United States

Habitat: Rivers, streams, and reservoirs

Diet: Insects, crayfish, snails, and fish

FUN FACT
Redbreast sunfish often build nests in groups of up to 80 nests.

REDEAR SUNFISH
(LEPOMIS MICROLOPHUS)

Redear sunfish are oval-shaped when viewed from the side. Their tails are slightly forked, and their snouts are pointed. Their upper bodies are usually olive green, and their bellies are white. Their sides are green or yellow. In males, the ear flap of this species has a red edge, giving the fish its name. Redear sunfish are bottom-dwellers that need warm waters with many aquatic plants. They are native to the southeastern United States but have been introduced throughout North America. They spawn in the spring or summer.

FUN FACT

Redear sunfish have been introduced in many places. They are stocked for fishing, but they also help lakes troubled by invasive species of snails or mollusks. These sunfish eat the invaders quickly.

HOW TO SPOT

Size: 8 to 11 inches (20.3 to 27.9 cm) long; 2 pounds (0.9 kg)
Range: United States, Mexico, and Puerto Rico
Habitat: Ponds, lakes, reservoirs, streams, and swamps
Diet: Snails, zooplankton, and larvae

ROCK BASS *(AMBLOPLITES RUPESTRIS)*

Rock bass are stocky fish with big mouths and red eyes. They have olive-green backs, gold sides, and white or silver bellies. Large spots run along their lower bodies. These sunfish live in clear, flowing streams with rocks or logs. They spawn in warm spring waters in abandoned nests of other sunfish. Their mottled appearance gives them camouflage in a rocky environment. They can also change colors quickly to blend in with their surroundings.

HOW TO SPOT

Size: 6 to 10 inches (15.2 to 25.4 cm) long; 1 pound (0.5 kg)
Range: Southern Canada and central and eastern United States
Habitat: Rivers, streams, and lakes
Diet: Insects, crayfish, and small fish

SMALLMOUTH BASS
(MICROPTERUS DOLOMIEU)

Smallmouth bass have smaller mouths than largemouth bass. These sunfish have dark-brown or green backs and sides with dark vertical bars. Their bellies are beige. Young fish have reddish tails with a dark vertical band. Smallmouth bass live in clear, cool, and fast-flowing water with few plants. They spawn in spring and summer. These fish are top predators in the food chain. They are very invasive when introduced to a new habitat, threatening prey such as fish, frogs, and invertebrates.

HOW TO SPOT

Size: 10 to 20 inches (25.4 to 50.8 cm) long; 1 to 3.5 pounds (0.5 to 1.6 kg)

Range: United States and southern Canada

Habitat: Lakes, rivers, and streams

Diet: Insects, frogs, fish, and invertebrates

FUN FACT
Smallmouth bass can be kept in home aquariums. But be careful—they are very aggressive fish that grab food that is offered.

SPOTTED BASS
(MICROPTERUS PUNCTULATUS)

Spotted bass are large fish with large mouths. Their upper bodies are green and mottled. Their lower sides and bellies are white with dark spots. A dark horizontal stripe runs across their sides, which also have dark spots. Spotted bass have a scattered range across the United States. They visit warm streams during spring spawning, returning to larger water habitats in the fall. Spotted bass catch prey by ambushing them from a hiding place and sucking them up. They are most active at dawn and dusk, often swimming at low depths.

HOW TO SPOT

Size: 10 to 17 inches (25.4 to 43.2 cm) long; 0.5 to 3.5 pounds (0.2 to 1.6 kg)

Range: Southern and central United States

Habitat: Rivers, streams, tributaries, and reservoirs

Diet: Insects, crayfish, and fish

WARMOUTH *(LEPOMIS GULOSUS)*

Warmouth are large sunfish with large mouths. They have mottled-brown bodies with gold bellies. Males have a bright-orange spot on their dorsal fins. Males also have red gill flaps and eyes that turn red during spawning. Warmouth are found across the United States. They lurk in weeds or under rocks in quiet waters, waiting for prey and avoiding predators such as large fish, herons, water snakes, and turtles. Spawning occurs in spring, and males defend their nests until their young hatch. Warmouth can hybridize with bluegill and green sunfish.

HOW TO SPOT

Size: 4 to 10 inches (10.2 to 25.4 cm) long; 2.3 pounds (1 kg)
Range: United States
Habitat: Lakes, swamps, streams, and ponds
Diet: Zooplankton, fish, mollusks, and insects

FUN FACT
Warmouth can survive in polluted waters with low oxygen levels where other sunfish cannot.

WHITE CRAPPIE *(POMOXIS ANNULARIS)*

White crappie are round when viewed from the side and have large mouths. They have silver-and-white bellies and silver-green backs. Their fins are checkered with dark spots, and vertical stripes run along their sides. Males develop darker throats during spring spawning. White crappie are native to the Mississippi River and Great Lakes regions but have been stocked throughout North America. Young fish stay in shallow, sun-drenched waters for their first three years. Then they join adults in schools in deeper waters.

HOW TO SPOT

Size: 6.7 to 21 inches (17 to 53.3 cm) long; 1 to 5 pounds (0.5 to 2.3 kg)

Range: United States and sourthern Canada

Habitat: Rivers, streams, lakes, and ponds

Diet: Insects, fish, and amphibians

FUN FACT
Male white crappies are very protective of their nests. They bite, push, and chase away intruders.

CHANGING FISH COLORS

Some freshwater fish change colors. Spawning males may change colors to attract females. Some change colors when stressed. Others have been observed changing colors when swimming from bright, sunlit waters to darker depths or as day turns into night. Colors are also affected by changes in season, diet, and habitat.

BLACK BULLHEAD *(AMEIURUS MELAS)*

Black bullheads have long, chubby bodies. Their backs are black, brown, or green. Their bellies are gray, yellow, or white. Despite their name, only young black bullheads are completely black. These catfish are found across North America because they have been stocked in many regions for sport fishing. They live mostly in cloudy, slow-moving waters. Spawning occurs in spring or summer, and both parents guard the nests. Young black bullheads eat mostly crustaceans, and adults add plants to their diet.

HOW TO SPOT

Size: 8 to 12 inches (20.3 to 30.5 cm) long; 2.3 pounds (1 kg)
Range: United States, southwestern Canada, and northern Mexico
Habitat: Streams and rivers
Diet: Insects, crustaceans, and plants

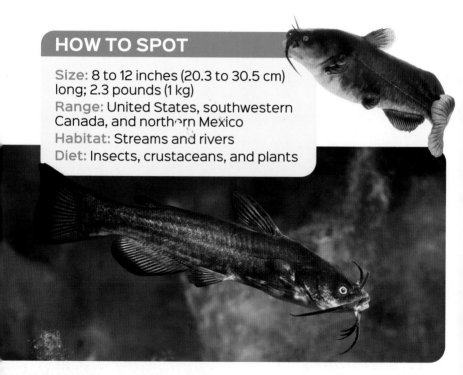

WHAT ARE CATFISH?

Catfish are fish with at least one pair of barbels. They belong to about 35 fish families. Most are freshwater species. They are bottom-dwellers that scavenge mostly at night. Many catfish have spines that release venom when disturbed. Catfish have no scales and are sometimes covered in bony plates.

BLUE CATFISH *(ICTALURUS FURCATUS)*

Blue catfish are the largest North American catfish. They have a flat dorsal fin and a forked tail fin. Their backs and sides are silver and blue. Their bellies are white. Blue catfish are native to the Mississippi, Missouri, Ohio, and Rio Grande River basins. They live in big rivers with fast-moving water, deep channels, and sandy bottoms. Spawning happens in the spring. They can survive in water with higher salinity than normal for freshwater habitats. Blue catfish are top predators in regions such as the Chesapeake Bay tributaries.

HOW TO SPOT

Size: 2 to 5 feet (0.6 to 1.5 m) long; 100 pounds (45.4 kg)

Range: Mexico; central, southern, eastern, and southeastern United States

Habitat: Rivers

Diet: Fish, insects, and plants

BROWN BULLHEAD
(AMEIURUS NEBULOSUS)

Brown bullheads have wide, flat heads. They also have square-shaped tail fins and sharp spines. Irregular rows of teeth are found on both jaws. Their bodies are olive green or yellowish brown. Their bellies are yellow or white. Brown bullheads are found widely in North America. They live in warm, muddy, and slow-moving waters with aquatic plants. These catfish can handle waters with higher salinity levels. Spawning occurs from spring to summer.

HOW TO SPOT

Size: 8 to 12 inches (20.3 to 30.5 cm) long; 1.1 pounds (0.5 kg)

Range: United States and eastern Canada

Habitat: Ponds, lakes, rivers, streams, and reservoirs

Diet: Insects, crustaceans, fish, and plants

FUN FACT
Both parents guard their young after hatching, chasing away fish that come close. If their young swim away, parents grab them with their mouths and bring them home.

CAROLINA MADTOM
(NOTURUS FURIOSUS)

Carolina madtoms are small, chubby catfish. They have mottled, yellow to dark-brown bodies. Three dark bands that look like saddles cross their backs. Yellow splotches are found between these bands. Brown bands mark their tail fins. Carolina madtoms are native to the Tar and Neuse River basins. They often live near woody debris. Spawning occurs from spring to summer. These fish need clean, flowing water to survive. Their population is declining because of climate change, water pollution, drought, and predation from species such as the flathead catfish.

HOW TO SPOT

Size: 5 inches (12.7 cm) long; 0.6 ounces (17 g)
Range: North Carolina in the United States
Habitat: Rivers
Diet: Larvae, insects, and invertebrates

CHANNEL CATFISH
(ICTALURUS PUNCTATUS)

Channel catfish have upper jaws that project beyond their lower jaws. Their sides are gray and blue. They have black backs and white bellies. Small, black spots cover their lower bodies. Channel catfish are the most abundant catfish species in North America. They live in large, slow-moving streams. Spawning occurs in spring or summer. Males build nests, guard them, and eat any damaged eggs. Young fish eat insects, plants, and small animals, while adults add snails and crustaceans to their diet.

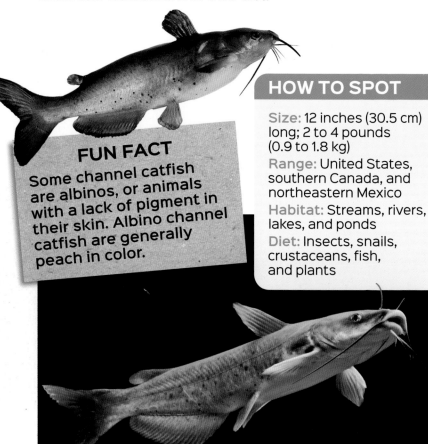

FUN FACT

Some channel catfish are albinos, or animals with a lack of pigment in their skin. Albino channel catfish are generally peach in color.

HOW TO SPOT

Size: 12 inches (30.5 cm) long; 2 to 4 pounds (0.9 to 1.8 kg)

Range: United States, southern Canada, and northeastern Mexico

Habitat: Streams, rivers, lakes, and ponds

Diet: Insects, snails, crustaceans, fish, and plants

CHUCKY MADTOM
(NOTURUS CRYPTICUS)

Chucky madtoms are small, slender catfish with rounded tail fins. Their bodies are brown or yellow gray. Yellow saddle marks run across their upper bodies. Black specks are found on their cheeks. Chucky madtoms live in clear, slow-moving waters, such as those in small- or medium-sized rocky creeks. They have been found only in Tennessee and Alabama. They live in the waters of Dunn Creek and Little Chucky Creek. Spawning happens in the spring or summer. Chucky madtoms are a highly threatened species. Pollution, farming, and introduced species such as crayfish have all led to their decline.

HOW TO SPOT

Size: 3 inches (7.6 cm) long; weight unknown
Range: Tennessee and Alabama in the United States
Habitat: Rivers and creeks
Diet: Insects and larvae

FLATHEAD CATFISH
(PYLODICTIS OLIVARIS)

Flathead catfish have wide, flat heads. Their lower jaws stick out, and their fins are slightly notched. Their backs are yellow to purplish brown. Their bellies are white to yellow. Young fish may have darker coloring. Their range stretches from the lower Great Lakes through the Mississippi River region to the Gulf states. They tend to live in deep pools with slow-moving, cloudy water. Spawning lasts from spring to summer. Unlike other catfish, they eat live prey. Young catfish eat worms, insects, and crayfish. Adults eat suckers, sunfish, largemouth bass, and even other flathead catfish.

HOW TO SPOT

Size: 3 to 4 feet (0.9 to 1.2 m) long; 100 pounds (45.4 kg)
Range: United States
Habitat: Streams, rivers, lakes, and reservoirs
Diet: Worms, insects, crayfish, and fish

FUN FACT
Male flatheads defend their nests, fanning out their tails to keep the eggs clean and give them more oxygen.

HEADWATER CATFISH
(ICTALURUS LUPUS)

Headwater catfish have rounded heads, forked tail fins, and projecting upper jaws. Their olive-green backs and sides have scattered, black spots. Their bellies are silver. Headwater catfish are native to the Rio Grande and Pecos River basins of Texas and New Mexico. These catfish live in the clear backwaters of rivers with sandy or rocky bottoms. They spawn in the spring or summer. Their greatest threats are competition and hybridization with channel catfish, which are causing their population to decline.

HOW TO SPOT

Size: 19 inches (48.2 cm) long; weight unknown

Range: Southwestern United States and northeastern Mexico

Habitat: Rivers and streams

Diet: Plants, fish, algae, crustaceans, and insects

FUN FACT
The headwater catfish is very similar to the channel catfish. Its main differences are a wider head, mouth, and snout.

51

SNAIL BULLHEAD
(AMEIURUS BRUNNEUS)

Snail bullheads have flat heads and rounded snouts. Their tail fins are short and rounded. They have yellow-brown to olive-green upper bodies and blue-and-white lower bodies. A large, dark spot marks their dorsal fin. They are native to rivers of Alabama and Georgia. Snail bullheads live in deep and fast-moving waters with sandy and rocky bottoms. Spawning occurs from spring to summer for longer periods than most catfish. Snail bullheads get their common name because their diet include snails.

FUN FACT

The word *ameiurus* in the snail bullhead's scientific name means "unforked" in Latin. It refers to this bullhead's unforked tail fin, which is rare for catfish.

HOW TO SPOT

Size: 10 to 12 inches (25.4 to 30.5 cm) long; 1.1 to 7.9 pounds (0.5 to 3.6 kg)
Range: Eastern and southern United States
Habitat: Rivers and streams
Diet: Phytoplankton, snails, crustaceans, and fish

STONECAT *(NOTURUS FLAVUS)*

Stonecats have rectangular tail fins. Their upper jaws project beyond their lower jaws. Their upper bodies are yellow and brown. Their bellies are light yellow or white. They live in fast-moving rivers and streams or rocky lakes. Spawning happens in the summer. Stonecats hide under rocks during the day and feed at night. Males guard the eggs and young until they can survive on their own. Young fish eat larvae. Adults also eat crayfish and fish. Their name refers to the stones they hide under, combined with the "cat" from catfish.

HOW TO SPOT

Size: 8 to 10 inches (20.3 to 25.4 cm) long; 0.2 to 1.1 pounds (0.1 to 0.5 kg)

Range: Southern Canada and midwestern and northeastern United States

Habitat: Streams, rivers, and lakes

Diet: Larvae, crayfish, and fish

TADPOLE MADTOM
(NOTURUS GYRINUS)

Tadpole madtoms are small and chubby. They look like tadpoles because their back fin is connected to the tail fin. Their backs and sides are tan or brown. A dark line runs across their bodies. Their bellies and fins are white or yellow. Tadpole madtoms live in shallow, slow-moving waters near aquatic plants. Spawning occurs in the summer. These fish hide during the day. At night, they feed on larvae, crustaceans, and worms. Sometimes small fish are added to their diet.

HOW TO SPOT

Size: 4.5 inches (11.4 cm) long; 0.6 ounces (17 g)

Range: Southeastern Canada and midwestern and eastern United States

Habitat: Rivers, lakes, and ponds

Diet: Larvae, crustaceans, worms, fish eggs, and fish

WHITE CATFISH *(AMEIURUS CATUS)*

White catfish have chubby bodies and forked tail fins. Their backs and upper sides are blue, gray, or black. They have white heads and mottled sides, white bellies, and dark fins. Their native range extends along the Atlantic coast from New York to Florida. White catfish live in slow-moving waters and can handle salt water. Spawning occurs from spring to summer. Unlike other catfish, they are most active at night. Young fish eat mostly insects. Adults add plants, fish, and invertebrates to their diet.

HOW TO SPOT

Size: 10 to 18 inches (25.4 to 45.7 cm) long; 0.5 to 3 pounds (0.2 to 1.4 kg)
Range: United States
Habitat: Ponds, rivers, and reservoirs
Diet: Insects, plants, invertebrates, and fish

VENOMOUS CATFISH

More than 1,000 catfish species are venomous, meaning they produce a harmful toxin. The venom is released through their spines when catfish are alarmed, such as when other fish come close or someone touches them. Species on other continents can kill humans with their venom, while stings from most North American venomous species are merely painful.

YAQUI CATFISH *(ICTALURUS PRICEI)*

Yaqui catfish are medium-sized catfish. Males have black upper bodies and gray lower bodies. Females and young fish have spotted, dark-gray upper bodies and white lower bodies. Yaqui catfish live in the drainages of the Rio Yaqui and Rio Casas Grandes, giving them their name. Yaqui catfish swim in calm, small- to medium-sized rivers over rocky or sandy bottoms. They spawn in the spring. Because of changing habitat conditions, these rare fish reproduce very little and have a low population.

HOW TO SPOT

Size: 15.7 inches (39.9 cm) long; 2.2 pounds (1 kg)
Range: Mexico; Arizona in the United States
Habitat: Rivers and streams
Diet: Insects, snails, plants, and fish

FUN FACT

Yaqui catfish are the only native catfish found west of the Continental Divide, which is the mountain range that separates North America's river systems.

YELLOW BULLHEAD
(AMEIURUS NATALIS)

Yellow bullheads have long, chubby bodies. Their upper jaw projects beyond their lower jaw. They have sharp teeth and spines. Their backs and sides are yellow and brown. Their bellies are yellow or white. Yellow bullheads are the most common bullhead catfish in the Ozarks and Bootheel lowland regions of Missouri. They live in clear, quiet, and slow-moving waters with aquatic plants or muddy waters with swift currents. Spawning occurs from spring to summer. Young fish eat larvae and small crustaceans. Adults add plants and fish to their diet.

FUN FACT

Eggs are guarded by the male yellow bullhead. After they hatch, he protects them until they are 2 inches (5.1 cm) long.

HOW TO SPOT

Size: 7 to 12 inches (17.8 to 30.5 cm) long; 0.2 to 1.3 pounds (0.1 to 0.5 kg)

Range: Southeastern Canada, central and eastern United States, and northern Mexico

Habitat: Streams and rivers

Diet: Larvae, crustaceans, crayfish, plants, and fish

BLUEBREAST DARTER
(ETHEOSTOMA CAMURUM)

Bluebreast darters are small fish with wide, rounded snouts. They have olive-green bodies with a light-colored stripe next to their dorsal fins. Their sides have red or brown spots. Spawning males have orange dorsal fins, red spots on their sides, and bright-blue breasts that give the species its name. Bluebreast darters live in fast-flowing waters with sandy or rocky bottoms. They migrate long distances for spring spawning, swimming from lower parts of a stream to parts very far upstream.

HOW TO SPOT

Size: 3 inches (7.6 cm) long; 4.8 to 9.6 oz (136 to 272.2 g)
Range: Midwestern and eastern United States
Habitat: Streams and rivers
Diet: Insects and larvae

FUN FACT

During spawning, male bluebreast darters choose sites around large stones. Females approach and lay eggs near the nest-stone.

WHAT ARE PERCH AND DARTERS?

Perch are a family of more than 200 fish species in the northern hemisphere. The soft and spiny sections of their dorsal fins are separated. Yellow perch and walleye are popular freshwater sport fish. Darters are tiny perch. Native to North America, they dart about stream and lake bottoms searching for food.

JOHNNY DARTER
(ETHEOSTOMA NIGRUM)

Johnny darters are especially tiny darters. They have yellow or brown bodies and white bellies. Their backs and sides have dark splotches in a W shape. Their tail fins have brown stripes. Spawning males turn black on their heads, upper bodies, and dorsal fins. Johnny darters are found in shallow, slow-moving waters. They spawn in warming spring waters and attach their eggs to the undersides of rocks. Males guard the eggs until they hatch, cleaning them with their fins up to 16 times per hour.

HOW TO SPOT

Size: 2.8 inches (7.1 cm) long; up to 0.1 ounces (2.8 g)

Range: Southeastern Canada and eastern and southeastern United States

Habitat: Streams, lakes, and rivers

Diet: Larvae and crustaceans

LOGPERCH *(PERCINA CAPRODES)*

Logperch have cone-shaped snouts. They get their name from the log shape of their bodies. Their backs and sides are olive green and yellow. Their bellies are white. Many brown stripes cross their backs. Their tail fins have a black spot. Logperch live in small- or medium-sized rivers and gravel shorelines in reservoirs. They use their snouts to lift up rocks when looking for prey such as crayfish, worms, and flies. Spawning occurs in the spring.

HOW TO SPOT

Size: 4 to 6 inches (10.2 to 15.2 cm) long; 0.3 to 0.6 ounces (8.5 to 17 g)

Range: Southeastern Canada and midwestern and eastern United States

Habitat: Rivers, streams, lakes, creeks, and reservoirs

Diet: Crayfish, worms, larvae, snails, and flies

RAINBOW DARTER
(ETHEOSTOMA CAERULEUM)

Rainbow darters are very colorful fish. These stout darters have light-brown bodies and darker-brown, mottled backs. Spawning males have bright blue-green stripes. Orange markings are found on their heads and between their stripes. Their fins are tipped with blue, green, and orange. Rainbow darters live in clear, rocky streams with mud-free bottoms. Spawning occurs in the spring. Young fish eat mostly small crustaceans. Adults add larvae, snails, and crayfish to their diet.

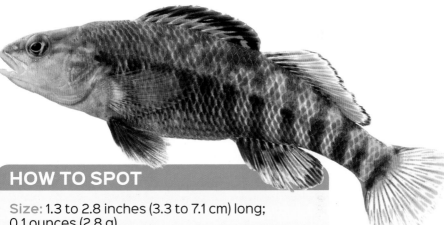

HOW TO SPOT

Size: 1.3 to 2.8 inches (3.3 to 7.1 cm) long; 0.1 ounces (2.8 g)
Range: Southeastern Canada; midwestern, southeastern, and eastern United States
Habitat: Streams and rivers
Diet: Larvae, snails, crayfish, and crustaceans

RUSH DARTER
(ETHEOSTOMA PHYTOPHILUM)

Rush darters are tiny darters. Their bodies are brown with dark vertical stripes. Rush darters are found in only a few creeks in Alabama. They need clear, cool waters. These darters live in still or slow-moving streams with aquatic plants. Spawning occurs in the spring. Rush darters are a rare and threatened species. They are protected by Alabama laws and cannot be fished. Threats to their survival include water pollution, habitat loss, climate change, and food competition with other fish species.

HOW TO SPOT

Size: 2 to 3 inches (5.1 to 7.6 cm) long; weight unknown

Range: Alabama in the United States

Habitat: Streams

Diet: Crustaceans and insects

SAUGER *(SANDER CANADENSIS)*

Saugers are slender perch with big mouths and forked tail fins. Their upper jaws extend to the edge of their eyes. Their scales are unusually tooth-like and rough. Their bodies are golden yellow to green with dark splotches on the sides. Saugers live mostly in large, fast-flowing streams of the Mississippi and Missouri Rivers and tributaries. They are sensitive to light, so they hide in plants and crevices or swim in shady areas. Spawning occurs in spring at night. Their strong eyesight helps them see in dark or cloudy waters.

FUN FACT

Saugers sometimes hybridize with walleye, creating "saugeye." These fish share traits with both species and are hard to identify.

HOW TO SPOT

Size: 12 to 15 inches (30.5 to 38.1 cm) long; 2.5 pounds (1.1 kg)
Range: United States
Habitat: Streams and rivers
Diet: Insects, crustaceans, and fish

SNAIL DARTER *(PERCINA TANASI)*

Snail darters have brown-and-green bodies with four black stripes on their backs. Spawning males turn blue and green on their sides and bellies. Spawning females turn gold. Snail darters live in clean, flowing waters with mud-free bottoms. They spawn in winter and spring in creeks with gravel bottoms. Snail darters often live near river darters and saddleback darters but do not compete with them for food. Their diet is rich in river snails, giving the snail darter its name.

HOW TO SPOT

Size: 2.5 to 3.5 inches (6.4 to 8.9 cm) long; weight unknown

Range: Southern United States

Habitat: Streams and rivers

Diet: River snails and larvae

FUN FACT

Snail darters were once a threatened species. Construction of a dam in Tennessee was paused for two years until the fish in those waters could be moved safely to another area.

64

SPECKLED DARTER
(ETHEOSTOMA STIGMAEUM)

Speckled darters have slender bodies. Their snouts are blunt, and their tail fins are rounded. Their bodies are light brown with several dark, saddle-shaped marks along the back. Spawning males have turquoise face markings and turquoise bars on their sides. Speckled darters swim in shallow, slow-moving waters of small- to medium-sized streams. They spawn in sandy or gravel-bottomed pools. While their population is stable, water pollution may threaten their species.

HOW TO SPOT

Size: 1.2 to 2 inches (3 to 5.1 cm) long; weight unknown
Range: Western and central United States
Habitat: Rivers and streams
Diet: Crustaceans and larvae

TESSELLATED DARTER
(ETHEOSTOMA OLMSTEDI)

Tessellated darters are slender fish. They have light-brown bodies with dark-brown, saddle-shaped marks across the backs. Dark-brown blotches mark their sides. Spawning males turn very dark. The tessellated darter's coloring acts as camouflage. These darters live in quiet pools within rivers and streams with sandy or muddy bottoms. They are also found in shallow lake areas. Spawning occurs in the winter or spring. Tessellated darters are very similar to Johnny darters and were once considered the same species.

HOW TO SPOT

Size: 1 to 3 inches (2.5 to 7.6 cm) long; weight unknown

Range: Southeastern Canada and eastern and southeastern United States

Habitat: Rivers, streams, and lakes

Diet: Larvae, crustaceans, snails, algae, and small fish

FUN FACT
These darters sometimes burrow under sand, exposing only their eyes and tail tips.

VARIEGATE DARTER

(ETHEOSTOMA VARIATUM)

Variegate darters are big and colorful darters. Red-orange, blue-green, and brown vertical bands run across their golden bodies. Scattered red spots are found near their tail fins. Males have blue-green tail fins. Spawning males have red-orange patches on the sides. Variegate darters live in the drainage basin of the Ohio River. They live in clear, fast-flowing waters. These darters are found in medium- to large-sized rivers with gravel or rock bottoms. Spawning occurs in the spring.

HOW TO SPOT

Size: 2.5 to 3.5 inches (6.4 to 8.9 cm) long; weight unknown
Range: Central and northeastern United States
Habitat: Rivers and streams
Diet: Insects

FUN FACT
After burying their eggs in gravel or sand, variegate darters leave the eggs alone. Young fish take care of themselves when they are born.

WALLEYE *(SANDER VITREUS)*

Walleye have big mouths with sharp teeth. Their bodies are gold and olive green with a white belly. Several black stripes run across the back. These perch live in cool, deep, calm waters. These fish rest during the day under logs, tree roots, and aquatic plants. They swim to shallow water at night to search for prey. Walleye spawn in the spring or summer. Their name refers to their unusually shiny eyes that seem to point outward—helping them see especially well at night.

HOW TO SPOT

Size: 30 to 36 inches (76.2 to 91.4 cm) long; 10 to 20 pounds (4.5 to 9.1 kg)

Range: Canada and United States

Habitat: Lakes, rivers, and reservoirs

Diet: Insects, fish, and invertebrates

YELLOW PERCH *(PERCA FLAVESCENS)*

Yellow perch have long, flat, yellow bodies. There are vertical olive-green stripes on their sides. Their eyes are green or yellow. Females are larger than males. Yellow perch can handle low oxygen levels but avoid cold and deep water. They live in clear, slow-moving waters with aquatic plants. Spawning occurs between winter and summer in the northern hemisphere and summer and fall in the southern hemisphere. Females lay many eggs that hatch when habitat conditions are right.

FUN FACT

Yellow perch have small teeth that slant backward and rakes on their gills. These features help them strain out food sources in the water.

HOW TO SPOT

Size: 3.9 to 10 inches (9.9 to 25.4 cm) long; 2 to 4 pounds (0.9 to 1.8 kg)

Range: United States and central Canada

Habitat: Ponds, lakes, and rivers

Diet: Invertebrates, fish, and zooplankton

BIGMOUTH BUFFALO
(ICTIOBUS CYPRINELLUS)

Bigmouth buffalo are the largest members of the sucker family. They have thick bodies and a large, slanted mouth that gives them their name. Their bodies are bronze or olive green with lighter-colored bellies. Spawning males are darker overall. These suckers live in slow-moving, clear rivers. Bigmouth buffalo frequent shallow waters in the spring and summer and deeper waters in the fall and winter. They sometimes migrate upstream during spring spawning to find water with aquatic plants. Bigmouth buffalo can live more than 100 years.

HOW TO SPOT

Size: 15 to 27 inches (38.1 to 68.6 cm) long; 2 to 14 pounds (0.9 to 6.4 kg)
Range: Southeastern Canada and midwestern and southern United States
Habitat: Streams, rivers, lakes, and reservoirs
Diet: Insects, phytoplankton, and crustaceans

WHAT ARE SUCKERS?

Suckers are a family of nearly 100 freshwater fish mostly native to North America. They have large, shiny scales and tooth-like structures in their throats that help with digestion. These slow-moving fish live at lake and river bottoms, sucking up plants and prey with their small, fleshy, downward-facing lips.

BLACK REDHORSE
(MOXOSTOMA DUQUESNEI)

Black redhorses have long, rounded snouts. Their upper bodies are gray or olive brown with hints of silver and blue. Their sides are silver and blue, and their bellies are white. They have gray or orange fins. They live in clean, fast-flowing waters with gravel, sand, or rock bottoms. These suckers cannot live in waters that have too much pollution, mud, or plant life. Black redhorses spawn in the spring. Young fish eat phytoplankton. Adults add crustaceans, worms, and insects to their diet.

HOW TO SPOT

Size: 10 to 15 inches (25.4 to 38.1 cm) long; 2.2 pounds (1 kg)

Range: Southeastern Canada and midwestern and southeastern United States

Habitat: Streams and rivers

Diet: Insects, crustaceans, and phytoplankton

FUN FACT
While most suckers have bumpy, V-shaped lips, black redhorses can be identified by their wrinkled, straight lips.

THE REDHORSE SUBSPECIES

Redhorses are a subspecies of suckers that are native to North America. Most have some red in their fins, which gives the subspecies its name. These suckers need fast-moving water to survive. Habitat changes such as water pollution from chemicals and excess mud can threaten redhorse subspecies.

CREEK CHUBSUCKER
(ERIMYZON OBLONGUS)

Creek chubsuckers are some of the smallest suckers. They have long bodies. The upper body is olive green to brown. The lower body is gold. Dark splotches cover the sides. Young fish have a dark lateral stripe instead. Creek chubsuckers swim in clear, slow-moving rivers and streams with muddy bottoms and aquatic plants. They spawn in fast-moving waters in the summer. After spawning, they migrate downstream to larger creeks. Their population is declining in streams that are too muddy from farming.

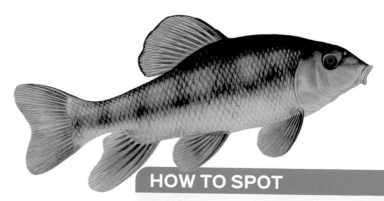

HOW TO SPOT

Size: 8 to 14 inches (20.3 to 35.6 cm) long; 8 to 9.6 ounces (226.8 to 272.2 g)

Range: Eastern and southeastern United States

Habitat: Streams, rivers, and lakes

Diet: Larvae and crustaceans

FUN FACT

Because creek chubsuckers are so sensitive to mud and sand, scientists monitor these fish to measure the water quality of their habitats.

GOLDEN REDHORSE
(MOXOSTOMA ERYTHRURUM)

Golden redhorses have a fairly large head for a redhorse, a short dorsal fin, and a forked tail fin. Their upper bodies are gold, and their lower bodies are silver. Their dorsal and tail fins are gray. The lower fins are orange. Golden redhorse are very common in the basins of the Missouri, Ohio, and Mississippi Rivers. They tend to live in pool areas in clear, flowing streams with rock or gravel bottoms. Golden redhorses spawn in the spring. They eat bottom-dwelling larvae, insects, and crustaceans.

FUN FACT

The body of the golden redhorse is tapered at both ends. Its shape allows it to swim against the current, helping it chase prey.

HOW TO SPOT

Size: 12 to 31 inches (30.5 to 78.7 cm) long; 1 to 5 pounds (0.5 to 2.3 kg)

Range: Southeastern and central Canada; midwestern and southeastern United States

Habitat: Streams, rivers, and lakes

Diet: Mollusks, phytoplankton, crustaceans, and insects

NORTHERN HOGSUCKER
(HYPENTELIUM NIGRICANS)

Northern hogsuckers are long, slender fish. They have a big, bony, and square-shaped head and a forked tail. They are named after their bumpy and pig-like snout. Northern hogsuckers have a yellow-and-green upper body and a white belly. Dark, saddle-shaped patches are often found on the upper body. They live in streams with fast-moving, clear waters. Spawning happens in the spring. Northern hogsuckers are nearly invisible when resting on gravel beds. These strong suckers flip over rocks and stir up mud to find food.

HOW TO SPOT

Size: 8 to 15 inches (20.3 to 38.1 cm) long; 2 pounds (0.9 kg)
Range: Southeastern Canada and midwestern and eastern United States
Habitat: Streams and rivers
Diet: Insects

NOTCHLIP REDHORSE
(MOXOSTOMA COLLAPSUM)

Notchlip redhorses are long fish with large scales. Their upper bodies are light brown or olive green, and their bellies are white. Their sides are silvery or golden. Females and spawning males have a dark stripe along the middle of their sides. Notchlip redhorses are widespread in several river systems ranging from Virginia to Georgia. These redhorses live in the slightly muddy waters of medium- to large-sized rivers. They spawn in the spring. Although the population is stable, potential threats include excessively muddy waters, food competition with other fish species, and predation by catfish species.

HOW TO SPOT

Size: 14 to 18 inches (35.6 to 45.7 cm) long; weight unknown
Range: Southern United States
Habitat: Rivers and lakes
Diet: Insects and mollusks

QUILLBACK *(CARPIODES CYPRINUS)*

Quillbacks are flat fish with small heads. They have long dorsal fins and a forked tail fin. Their bodies are silver or bronze. Their tails and lower fins are white. They live mostly in clear, deep, fast-moving waters but can adapt to slower-moving waters. These suckers spawn in the spring. Young fish are common prey for other fish. Quillbacks are a threatened species in some regions.

HOW TO SPOT

Size: 12 to 20 inches (30.5 to 50.8 cm) long; 0.8 to 2.3 pounds (0.4 to 1 kg)

Range: Canada, Mexico, and midwestern and eastern United States

Habitat: Streams, rivers, and lakes

Diet: Insects, phytoplankton, clams, and snails

FUN FACT

Quillbacks get their name from the long, projecting rays on their back fins that look like quill pens.

SHORTHEAD REDHORSE
(MOXOSTOMA MACROLEPIDOTUM)

Shorthead redhorses are slender suckers with a short dorsal fin. Their heads are shorter than those of other redhorse sucker species. They have an olive-green and brown upper body. The sides are golden yellow, and the belly is white. They have an olive-green dorsal fin, a red tail fin, and orange lower fins. Shorthead redhorses are most common in rivers with clear, fast-flowing water and gravel and sand bottoms. They can also handle cloudy waters. Spawning occurs in the spring.

HOW TO SPOT

Size: 9 to 30 inches (22.9 to 76.2 cm) long; 1 to 5 pounds (0.5 to 2.3 kg)

Range: Southeastern Canada and midwestern and southeastern United States

Habitat: Streams, rivers, and lakes

Diet: Larvae, insects, mollusks, and worms

SILVER REDHORSE
(MOXOSTOMA ANISURUM)

Silver redhorses are long, slender fish with a forked tail. They have a green-blue to brown back and undersides. Their sides are yellow, and their dorsal and tail fins are gray. Their other fins are orange or beige. These suckers are native to the Great Lakes and the Mississippi and St. Lawrence River basins. They live in clear streams and rivers with a strong, steady flow and gravel or rock bottoms. Spawning occurs in the spring.

HOW TO SPOT

Size: 12 to 28 inches (30.5 to 71.1 cm) long; 2 to 10 pounds (0.9 to 4.5 kg)

Range: Southeastern and central Canada and midwestern and eastern United States

Habitat: Streams, rivers, and lakes

Diet: Larvae, insects, phytoplankton, and clams

FUN FACT

Where the silver redhorse is present, water quality will tend to be high; the fish cannot live in murky waters.

WHITE SUCKER
(CATOSTOMUS COMMERSONII)

White suckers are long fish with a forked tail fin. They have an olive-green upper body and beige belly. These suckers have a large range. It covers much of Canada and the Great Lakes. They live in clear, cold, shallow waters. Spawning occurs in the spring. White suckers are highly adaptable fish. They can handle changing water conditions such as mud, pollution, and low oxygen levels better than most freshwater fish. White suckers eat mostly worms and small crustaceans when young. Adults add zooplankton and insects to their diet.

HOW TO SPOT

Size: 12 to 20 inches (30.5 to 50.8 cm) long; 1 to 2 pounds (0.5 to 0.9 kg)
Range: Canada and the Great Lakes
Habitat: Lakes, rivers, and streams
Diet: Invertebrates, crustaceans, zooplankton, and insects

STRIPED BASS *(MORONE SAXATILIS)*

Striped bass are long fish with slightly arched backs. They have a light-green or brown body and a white belly. Dark horizontal stripes run across the sides. Striped bass are anadromous. Some spend most of their adult lives in salt water, while others spend this time in rivers. They spawn in the spring in running fresh water. When landlocked due to dam construction, striped bass can adapt to freshwater habitats. Striped bass eat zooplankton and larvae when young. Adults eat fish, crustaceans, and mollusks.

HOW TO SPOT

Size: 24 to 36 inches (61 to 91.4 cm) long; 10 to 30 pounds (4.5 to 13.6 kg)
Range: United States and southeastern Canada
Habitat: Rivers, lakes, and estuaries
Diet: Zooplankton, larvae, mollusks, crustaceans, and fish

WHAT ARE TRUE BASS?

While certain sunfish have the name "bass," they are not actual bass. True bass are members of the Moronidae family. Some are saltwater fish, while others are freshwater species. They are silvery, stout, flat fish with a large mouth and forked tail. They often swim and feed in schools.

WHITE BASS *(MORONE CHRYSOPS)*

White bass have arched backs that are blue and gray. The sides are silver and white with yellow on the lower edges. Gray-brown or black horizontal stripes cross the back. Large populations are found in the clear waters of the Mississippi River and the Great Lakes. In winter or spring, they migrate upstream in a river or to a freshwater lake to spawn.

FUN FACT

The word *chrysops* in the white bass' scientific name refers to its golden eye. In Greek, *chrys* means "gold" and *ops* means "eye."

HOW TO SPOT

Size: 9 to 15 inches (22.9 to 38.1 cm) long; 3 to 5 pounds (1.4 to 2.3 kg)
Range: United States
Habitat: Lakes and rivers
Diet: Zooplankton, insects, crustaceans, and fish

WHITE PERCH *(MORONE AMERICANA)*

White perch are not related to other perch. They have long, chubby, silver bodies with two dorsal fins separated by a small notch. Lateral stripes appear when the fish are young and are lost in adulthood. Their backs are olive green to black, their bellies are silver and white, and their fins are gray. They are native to the Atlantic coast of North America. White perch are semi-anadromous. In the spring, they migrate upstream from salty estuaries to fresh water for spawning.

HOW TO SPOT

Size: 8 to 15 inches (20.3 to 38.1 cm) long; 1 to 2 pounds (0.5 to 0.9 kg)

Range: Southeastern Canada and eastern United States

Habitat: Ponds, rivers, bays, tributaries, and lakes

Diet: Larvae, crustaceans, insects, and fish

YELLOW BASS
(MORONE MISSISSIPPIENSIS)

Yellow bass are small bass. Their bodies are yellow and silver with dark stripes. Yellow bass are not an abundant fish but are still common in their native Mississippi River and Lake Michigan habitats. Yellow bass live in clear to slightly cloudy water with a rock, mud, sand, or gravel bottom. They spawn in the spring in moving waters. Yellow bass reproduce quickly and in large numbers, with eggs hatching in just four to six days.

HOW TO SPOT

Size: 12 to 18 inches (30.5 to 45.7 cm) long; 1 pound (0.5 kg)
Range: Midwestern and southern United States
Habitat: Lakes, rivers, and reservoirs
Diet: Insects, crustaceans, and small fish

FUN FACT
Adults often eat their recently hatched young.

CHAIN PICKEREL *(ESOX NIGER)*

Chain pickerel have light-green bodies. Yellow-and-green, scattered markings cover the body. The tail fin is forked. Chain pickerel live in warm, shallow, slow-moving fresh waters. Sometimes they swim toward salty waters in the winter. Spawning occurs in early spring. They spawn earlier than other local fish, which allows their young to eat the young of other fish species. Young chain pickerel eat small fish until they grow big enough to grab larger prey such as ducks, snakes, and muskrats.

HOW TO SPOT

Size: 14 to 19 inches (35.6 to 48.2 cm) long; 2 to 4 pounds (0.9 to 1.8 kg)

Range: Canada and midwestern and southern United States

Habitat: Lakes, swamps, rivers, and streams

Diet: Fish, snakes, frogs, ducks, and muskrats

WHAT ARE PIKE?

Pike belong to the Esocidae family. Muskellunge and pickerel are native North American species. Pike have long bodies, small scales, a shovel-shaped snout, and a big mouth with powerful teeth. Because the dorsal fin is so close to the tail, pike can move quickly by whipping their tail. They often hunt alone, staying still in weedy waters and grabbing prey that come close.

GRASS PICKEREL
(ESOX AMERICANUS VERMICULATUS)

Grass pickerel have an olive-green or yellow-brown upper body that is mottled in dark green. Their belly is beige, and their tail is forked. Grass pickerel live mostly in warm, clear, shallow waters with aquatic plants. They also live in habitats with muddy or rocky bottoms. Grass pickerel spawn in the spring. Young fish eat insects and crustaceans. Adults add fish such as darters and sunfish to their diet. They are a subspecies of the redfin pickerel.

HOW TO SPOT

Size: 10 to 12 inches (25.4 to 30.5 cm) long; 12.8 ounces (362.9 g)

Range: Canada and midwestern and eastern United States

Habitat: Ponds, streams, and lakes

Diet: Insects, crustaceans, crayfish, and fish

FUN FACT
Like other pickerel, grass pickerel do not protect their eggs or their young.

85

MUSKELLUNGE *(ESOX MASQUINONGY)*

Muskellunge, also called muskies, have a silver upper body and a white belly with dark blotches. They are native to the Mississippi River, Great Lakes, St. Lawrence River, and Hudson Bay areas. These fish live mostly in cool, clear, shallow, slow-moving waters. As adults, they sometimes spend time in deeper waters. They seldom leave their home range except to spawn in the spring. Muskellunge can jump in the air at speeds of up to 30 miles per hour (48.3 kmh).

HOW TO SPOT

Size: 3.3 to 4.7 feet (1 to 1.4 m) long; 10 to 40 pounds (4.5 to 18.1 kg)
Range: Canada and United States
Habitat: Rivers, streams, and lakes
Diet: Fish, rodents, waterfowl, and muskrats

NORTHERN PIKE *(ESOX LUCIUS)*

Northern pike have a green or brown upper body and a white belly. Rows of white-yellow spots cover the body. The dorsal and tail fins are green, yellow, or orange. Northern pike live in the cold, slow waters of rivers or lakes. They eat fish such as yellow perch, suckers, sunfish, and other pike. They also eat ducks, rodents, snakes, and frogs. Northern pike spawn in the spring after ice melts in their habitat. Like other pike, they scatter their eggs, which attach to aquatic plants and wait to hatch.

HOW TO SPOT

Size: 16 to 22 inches (40.6 to 55.9 cm) long; 5 to 10 pounds (2.3 to 4.5 kg)
Range: Canada and United States
Habitat: Rivers and lakes
Diet: Ducks, fish, frogs, rodents, and snakes

FUN FACT

Some Northern pike can grow to more than 62 pounds (28.1 kg)! Northern pike that are more than 20 pounds (9.1 kg) are trophy fish.

REDFIN PICKEREL
(ESOX AMERICANUS)

Redfin pickerel have a brown or beige upper body and a white belly. Dark-green, wavy bars run across their sides. Their fins are red, yellow, or brown, and their tails are forked. Redfin pickerel live mostly in the calm backwaters of ponds and streams with aquatic plants. They are rarely found in main bodies of big rivers or lakes. Spawning occurs in the spring in shallow waters. Redfin pickerel sometimes hybridize with chain pickerel.

HOW TO SPOT

Size: 8 to 16 inches (20.3 to 40.6 cm) long; 1 to 2 pounds (0.5 to 0.9 kg)

Range: Canada and southern and eastern United States

Habitat: Rivers, lakes, ponds, and swamps

Diet: Larvae, crayfish, and fish

TIGER MUSKELLUNGE
(ESOX MASQUINONGY X ESOX LUCIUS)

Commonly called tiger muskies, these fish are a hybrid of northern pike and muskellunge. They have long, cylindrical bodies. Their heads are long and flattened, and their jaws are shaped like a duck bill. Their bodies are silvery with stripes and spots in a vertical, tiger-like pattern. Tiger muskies live in cold, still waters. Their habitats range from deep waters to shallow waters with plants. They often hide in brush, waiting to pounce on prey that swims by.

HOW TO SPOT

Size: 1.5 to 4 feet (0.5 to 1.2 m) long; 1 to 18 pounds (0.5 to 8.2 kg)
Range: Canada and United States
Habitat: Rivers, streams, and lakes
Diet: Fish, rodents, frogs, and waterfowl

FUN FACT
Tiger muskies can't reproduce. Some are bred and stocked as game fish that can weigh more than 40 pounds (18.1 kg).

89

ALABAMA SHAD *(ALOSA ALABAMAE)*

Alabama shad are elongated, with a forked tail and projecting lower jaw. Their upper bodies are blue and green with hints of silver. Their lower bodies and bellies are silver or white. Females are larger than males. These shad spawn in the spring in fast-moving waters over gravel or sand. They eat very little during spawning, and many die afterward. They have a row of bony teeth on their tongue and rakes near the gills that help them grab and eat prey.

HOW TO SPOT

Size: 12 to 18 inches (30.5 to 45.7 cm) long; 3 pounds (1.4 kg)
Range: Southern United States
Habitat: Rivers, streams, and oceans
Diet: Insects and small fish

WHAT ARE SHAD AND HERRING?

Shad and herring belong to the Clupeidae family. These particular species are anadromous, spending much of their lives in salt water and returning to fresh water to spawn. They are fast and strong swimmers that travel in schools. The alosine and gizzard shad subfamilies include a total of 10 North American species.

ALEWIFE *(ALOSA PSEUDOHARENGUS)*

Alewives are long, silvery fish with gray-and-green backs. A dark spot is found behind their heads. Alewives are native to the East Coast rivers and streams that drain into the Atlantic Ocean. Spawning occurs in the spring. Young alewives grow so quickly that most swim to the ocean by their first fall. Alewives often feed at the water surface at night. Their rounded bellies may have given them their name—during the Middle Ages, female tavern keepers who made ale often had rounded bellies.

HOW TO SPOT

Size: 9 to 11 inches (22.9 to 27.9 cm) long; less than 1 pound (0.5 kg)

Range: Northeastern Canada and eastern United States

Habitat: Rivers, streams, and oceans

Diet: Zooplankton, shrimp, crustaceans, fish eggs, and fish

AMERICAN SHAD *(ALOSA SAPIDISSIMA)*

American shad have a deeply forked tail. Their bodies are metallic blue or green with dark spots on the shoulders. Females are generally larger than males. Spawning occurs in the spring in the same freshwater region where they were born. After spawning, adults die or return to the ocean. By their first fall, young fish leave their freshwater habitat and swim to the ocean where they live several years before spawning in fresh water. The American shad population has declined due to pollution, overfishing, and dam construction.

HOW TO SPOT

Size: 20 to 30 inches (50.8 to 76.2 cm) long; 12 pounds (5.4 kg)

Range: Canada, United States, and Mexico

Habitat: Rivers, streams, and oceans

Diet: Zooplankton, phytoplankton, crustaceans, and fish

FUN FACT

Just before spawning season begins, American shad eat heavily. During their upstream spawning migration journey, adults do not feed at all.

OVERFISHING AND STOCKING?

Overfishing can threaten freshwater fish populations. For this reason, some species are raised in fish hatcheries and stocked—or released—into suitable habitats. This stabilizes their population while allowing people to fish. However, stocking fish in non-native habitats can threaten a region's native animals through predation and food competition.

BLUEBACK HERRING
(ALOSA AESTIVALIS)

Blueback herring are small, silvery fish with a blue back and dark spots on the shoulders. Their bellies are white, and their fins are yellow green. These herring spawn in the spring in fresh or brackish—or somewhat salty—waters over gravel, sand, or plant surfaces. When their young hatch, they remain in fresh water throughout the summer until the waters cool. At that time, they swim downstream to salt water. The total number of marks on a blueback herring's scales indicates how many times it has spawned.

FUN FACT
When blueback herring migrate to the ocean for the first time, they may swim as far as 1,200 miles (1,931 km).

HOW TO SPOT

Size: 11 to 15 inches (27.9 to 38.1 cm) long; less than 1 pound (0.5 kg)
Range: Southeastern Canada and eastern United States
Habitat: Rivers, streams, and oceans
Diet: Zooplankton, crustaceans, and fish eggs

HICKORY SHAD *(ALOSA MEDIOCRIS)*

Hickory shad have a projecting lower jaw and a deeply forked tail. Their upper bodies are gray and green, and their sides are silver. Their bellies are white, and their shoulders have dark spots. In the spring, they return to their freshwater birthplace to spawn between dusk and midnight. Spawning takes place in many habitats, from backwaters to tidal areas of rivers. After spawning, adults die or return to the ocean.

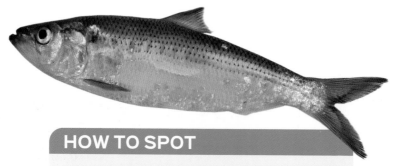

HOW TO SPOT

Size: 15 to 20 inches (38.1 to 50.8 cm) long; 2 pounds (0.9 kg)
Range: Eastern United States
Habitat: Rivers, streams, and oceans
Diet: Small fish, fish eggs, and crustaceans

THREADFIN SHAD
(DOROSOMA PETENENSE)

Threadfin shad are small, flat fish with a deeply forked tail. Their bodies are silver with a purple spot near the gills. All fins except the dorsal fin are yellow. Threadfin shad live in warm, fast-moving waters. They can handle salt water, but they cannot survive in cold waters below 45°F (7.2°C). They spawn in the spring and summer over plants in shallow shoreline areas. Rakes on their gills help them filter out rocks as they sweep bottom surfaces for food.

HOW TO SPOT

Size: 5 to 6 inches (12.7 to 15.2 cm) long; weight unknown

Range: Southern United States

Habitat: Rivers and reservoirs

Diet: Phytoplankton and zooplankton

FUN FACT
Some young threadfin shad mature so quickly that they can spawn in the same year they were born.

95

BLACKCHIN SHINER
(NOTROPIS HETERODON)

Blackchin shiners have large eyes and a pointed snout, lower jaw, and chin. Their upper bodies are brown and olive green, and their bellies are yellow with dark speckles. A dark zigzag pattern runs across the sides. These minnows live in cool, clear, shallow waters, such as those in lakes or slow-moving streams and rivers with aquatic plants and sandy bottoms. Spawning occurs in the spring and summer. Their population is threatened by changing water conditions and habitat loss because they cannot survive in salty or muddy waters.

HOW TO SPOT

Size: 5 to 7 inches (12.7 to 17.8 cm) long; 1 to 2.4 ounces (27.2 to 68 g)
Range: Midwestern and eastern United States
Habitat: Streams, rivers, and lakes
Diet: Crustaceans and insects

FUN FACT

Blackchin shiners eat a wider variety of foods than other minnows. They take half of their food from water surfaces and half from plants and bottom surfaces.

WHAT ARE MINNOWS?

Minnow is the common name for fish of the Cyprinidae family. They are the largest freshwater fish family in the world, with 270 North American species. These generally small fish have a single dorsal fin, a forked or curved tail fin, no teeth, and no scales on the head.

BLUNTNOSE MINNOW
(PIMEPHALES NOTATUS)

Bluntnose minnows are long, slender fish with a blunt nose. Their bodies are silver with hints of green and blue. A dark stripe runs from their snouts to their tails. Males darken during spawning. Bluntnose minnows live in lakes or clear, rocky, shallow streams and rivers. Spawning occurs from spring through summer. Like other minnows, they release a chemical when they are attacked by predators. Scientists think the pheromone attracts other competing predators that can startle the first one, giving these minnows a chance to swim away.

HOW TO SPOT

Size: 1.5 to 3.5 inches (3.8 to 8.9 cm) long; less than 0.1 ounces (2.8 g)

Range: Southeastern Canada, midwestern and southern United States, and the Great Lakes

Habitat: Streams, rivers, and lakes

Diet: Phytoplankton, larvae, crustaceans, fish eggs, and fish

PHEROMONES

Many fish release chemicals called pheromones that other fish can smell. Pheromones are released when a fish needs to communicate with other fish. Pheromones may be released to attract mates, signal to others during migration, indicate nearby prey, or warn about lurking predators.

BRIDLE SHINER *(NOTROPIS BIFRENATUS)*

Bridle shiners are narrow fish with a large, forked tail and large eyes. They have a golden body and a white belly. Their scales are diamond shaped. A black lateral stripe extends from their snout to their tail. Bridle shiners live by the shorelines of ponds and lakes as well as slow-moving streams with aquatic plants and muddy bottoms. They spawn in late spring or early summer. Bridle shiner populations are threatened. Their small size makes them easy prey for predators such as largemouth bass.

HOW TO SPOT

Size: 1 to 2 inches (2.5 to 5.1 cm) long; 0.02 to 0.03 ounces (0.45 to 0.9 g)
Range: Eastern Canada and eastern United States
Habitat: Rivers, streams, lakes, and ponds
Diet: Zooplankton and invertebrates

FUN FACT

Unlike other minnows, bridle shiners do not glide in water. Instead, they have a distinctive stop and start movement.

98

CENTRAL STONEROLLER
(CAMPOSTOMA ANOMALUM)

Central stonerollers have small eyes and a flat, extending lower jaw used to remove algae from rocks. They have an olive-green upper body and a white belly. These minnows live in cool, clear pools or streams with fast currents over rocky bottoms. They spawn in early spring. Males build nests by using their bodies to roll away large stones and form shallow pits for eggs, giving these fish their "stoneroller" name. They swim in schools and feed together along bottom surfaces. Central stonerollers are most active during the day, sometimes leaping along the water's surface.

HOW TO SPOT

Size: 3 to 6.5 inches (7.6 to 16.5 cm) long; 1.6 to 11.2 ounces (45.4 to 317.5 g)
Range: Southeastern Canada, central and eastern United States, and Mexico
Habitat: Streams and rivers
Diet: Phytoplankton

COMMON CARP *(CYPRINUS CARPIO)*

Common carp are the largest minnows. They have a blunt nose and barbels on both sides of their upper jaw. Their dorsal fin is long, and their tail fin is forked. Their upper body is green, yellow, or brown, and their belly is yellowish white. Common carp are native to Europe and Asia but have been widely introduced across North America. They live in slow-moving or still water with sandy bottoms. Spawning occurs from spring to summer. Common carp dig up roots along bottom surfaces, looking for food to eat.

HOW TO SPOT

Size: 12 to 25 inches (30.5 to 63.5 cm) long; 8 to 10 pounds (3.6 to 4.5 kg)

Range: Canada and United States

Habitat: Rivers, lakes, streams, estuaries, and reservoirs

Diet: Zooplankton, plants, invertebrates, snails, and fish

FUN FACT

Common carp are an invasive species. They disrupt the habitats of many native fish and waterfowl.

COMMON SHINER
(LUXILUS CORNUTUS)

Common shiners have a blunt snout and forked tail. Their upper body is olive green, and their lower body is silver and white. A wide, dark stripe runs along the body. Dark, moon-shaped marks are found on the sides. Spawning males have blue heads, a pink body, and golden stripes. Spawning occurs in spring and early summer. During this time, males use their snouts to dig pits for eggs. Several males may share the same nest area. These minnows swim in schools in small, clear streams with gravel and rock bottoms.

HOW TO SPOT

Size: 3 to 5 inches (7.6 to 12.7 cm) long; 1.6 to 11.2 ounces (45.4 to 317.5 g)

Range: Southern Canada and midwestern and eastern United States

Habitat: Streams and rivers

Diet: Insects, crustaceans, phytoplankton, and fish

CUTLIP MINNOW
(EXOGLOSSUM MAXILLINGUA)

Cutlip minnows are long fish with a rounded snout and slightly forked tail. They have a lower jaw with three lobes. Their body is olive green, and their belly is white. All fins are yellow except the reddish-brown dorsal fin. Cutlip minnows live in warm, clear, slow-moving waters with rock or gravel bottoms. Spawning occurs from spring to summer. These minnows are bottom-dwellers that eat aquatic insects. Threats to the species include habitat loss, competition for nest sites with other fish, and water pollution from farming.

HOW TO SPOT

Size: 3 to 4 inches (7.6 to 10.2 cm) long; 0.2 to 0.3 ounces (5.7 to 8.5 g)
Range: Southeastern Canada and northeastern United States
Habitat: Rivers, streams, and lakes
Diet: Insects and mollusks

FUN FACT
The cutlip minnow's lower lip has a dent in the middle, giving the species its name.

EMERALD SHINER
(NOTROPIS ATHERINOIDES)

Emerald shiners have long, slender, flat bodies. They have a rounded snout and large eyes. Their entire body is silver with a hint of emerald green, giving these fish their name. Emerald shiners are native to the Missouri and Yellowstone River basins. They swim in schools in rivers and open waters. These minnows typically stay near the water surface and avoid areas with aquatic plants. Spawning occurs in late spring or early summer. Young fish eat zooplankton, while adults add fish eggs and insect larvae to their diet.

HOW TO SPOT

Size: 3 to 6.5 inches (7.6 to 16.5 cm) long; up to 0.1 ounces (2.8 g)
Range: United States and southeastern Canada
Habitat: Streams, rivers, and lakes
Diet: Zooplankton, fish eggs, and insect larvae

FUN FACT
In some parts of the United States, emerald shiners have been introduced as food for larger fish.

103

FATHEAD MINNOW
(PIMEPHALES PROMELAS)

Fathead minnows are chubby fish. They have a blunt and rounded snout, short and rounded fins, and a dark stripe along their sides. They have green or olive bodies and yellow bellies. Fathead minnows live in schools near stream bottoms and pools of small creeks. Spawning occurs from spring to summer when males release a chemical that attracts females. Fathead minnows can handle high temperatures, low oxygen, and murky waters. They are most abundant in areas where they are the only fish species.

HOW TO SPOT

Size: 1.5 to 3 inches (3.8 to 7.6 cm) long; 0.2 ounces (5.7 g)
Range: United States and southeastern Canada
Habitat: Streams and creeks
Diet: Algae, insects, and crustaceans

FUN FACT
Female fathead minnows may spawn more than 12 times in a single summer, laying more than 4,000 eggs.

GOLDEN SHINER
(NOTEMIGONUS CRYSOLEUCAS)

Golden shiners are minnows with small, upturned mouths and forked tails. Adults are brassy gold, while young fish are silver with a dark lateral stripe. Males turn deep gold during spawning, which takes place throughout the spring and summer. Golden shiners have a very wide range throughout North America. They are found in nearly every lake and river in some parts of the eastern United States. These minnows live in deep, still, or slow-moving waters of swamps, lakes, ponds, rivers, and creeks.

HOW TO SPOT

Size: 3 to 9 inches (7.6 to 22.9 cm) long; 1.5 pounds (0.7 kg)

Range: Southeastern Canada and eastern and midwestern United States

Habitat: Lakes, swamps, and ponds

Diet: Zooplankton, phytoplankton, and small crustaceans

SPOTFIN SHINER
(CYPRINELLA SPILOPTERA)

Spotfin shiners are long, flat fish. Their upper bodies and backs are silver and blue with a dark stripe on each side. Their lower fins are yellow. Spawning males have dark dorsal fins. Spotfin shiners are found in clear creeks or rivers over sand and gravel. They can also handle muddy waters most of the time. Spawning occurs from spring until summer. Spotfin shiners usually feed near the bottom of streams and rivers during the day and near the surface at night.

HOW TO SPOT

Size: 2 to 5 inches (5.1 to 12.7 cm) long; weight unknown

Range: Southeastern Canada and midwestern, eastern, and southeastern United States

Habitat: Rivers, lakes, and reservoirs

Diet: Insects, plants, and small fish

SWALLOWTAIL SHINER
(NOTROPIS PROCNE)

Swallowtail shiners have a pointed or rounded snout and forked tail. Their breast has no scales. These minnows have an olive-green to yellow body with a dark-blue lateral stripe. Swallowtail shiners can handle muddy waters but avoid deep, fast-moving water. They live in warm, upland streams and the pools of small rivers. Spawning occurs from spring to summer over gravel and sand. These fish are usually found in schools near the water's bottom.

HOW TO SPOT

Size: 1.8 to 3.1 inches (4.6 to 7.9 cm) long; weight unknown

Range: Eastern and southeastern United States

Habitat: Streams, rivers, and lakes

Diet: Phytoplankton, insects, and worms

GLOSSARY

anadromous
Traveling up rivers from the ocean to breed.

camouflage
An animal's coloring or marks that help it blend in with its surroundings.

crustacean
An animal that has a hard outer covering and two pairs of antennae.

dorsal
Located near or on the back.

estuary
An area at the end of a river between land and the ocean.

food web
A group of many food chains that interact in an ecosystem.

hatchery
A place for hatching eggs.

invertebrate
An animal without a backbone.

phytoplankton
A microscopic plant in the ocean that provides food for marine species.

reservoir
A human-made lake where water is stored for use.

salinity
The amount of salt in water.

scavenge
To feed on decaying or dead matter.

stock
To release a fish species into a body of water to create or supplement populations of that species.

tributary
A river or stream that flows into and joins a larger river

vertebrate
An animal with a backbone.

zooplankton
A microscopic animal or animal-like organism that many fish and other animals eat.

TO LEARN MORE

FURTHER READINGS

Hamilton, S. L. *Sturgeon*. Abdo, 2015.

Mazzarella, Kerri. *Freshwater Fishing*. Crabtree Publishing, 2023.

Sullivan, Laura. *Saltwater and Freshwater Creatures Explained.* Cavendish Square Publishing, 2017.

ONLINE RESOURCES

To learn more about freshwater fish, please visit **abdobooklinks.com** or scan this QR code. These links are routinely monitored and updated to provide the most current information available.

PHOTO CREDITS

Cover Photos: Animal Search/Shutterstock Images, front (rainbow darter); Edvard Ellric/Shutterstock Images, front (pike perch); grey_and/Shutterstock Images, front (rainbow trout); milart/Shutterstock Images, front (bullhead); RLS Photo/Shutterstock Images, front (Acadian redfish, chain pickerel, pumpkinseed sunfish, smallmouth bass), back (lake trout); Thomas Hasenberger/Shutterstock Images, front (sturgeon); Dan Thornberg/Shutterstock Images, front (bluegill); Alexander Raths/Shutterstock Images, back (rainbow trout)

Interior Photos: slowmotiongli/Shutterstock Images, 1 (top left), 17 (top), 50 (bottom); Dan Thornberg/Shutterstock Images, 1 (middle left), 5 (top right), 21 (top), 29 (top), 30 (top), 112 (bottom); M Huston/Shutterstock Images, 1 (middle right), 89 (bottom); Botond1977/Shutterstock Images, 1 (bottom left), 23 (top); Animal Search/Shutterstock Images, 1 (bottom right), 61 (top); Robert Aguilar/Smithsonian Environmental Research Center/Flickr, 4, 42, 54 (top), 55, 57, 66, 75, 82, 88 (bottom), 91 (top), 92, 93, 94 (top), 95 (top), 95 (bottom), 99 (top), 101 (top), 102, 105, 107; FedBul/Shutterstock Images, 4–5, 33 (right); Ellen Edmonson and Hugh Chrisp/Wikimedia Commons, 5 (top left), 72 (top), 73, 74 (top), 77 (top), 79, 98; Edvard Ellric/Shutterstock Images, 5 (bottom), 69, 112 (left); Aleksander Hunta/Shutterstock Images, 8, 112 (top); Kevin Wells Photography/Shutterstock Images, 9 (top); Westend61/Getty Images, 9 (bottom); Kevin Kass/Shutterstock Images, 10; Shpatak/Shutterstock Images, 11 (top); The Old Major/Shutterstock Images, 11 (bottom); Cavan Images/Getty Images, 12; Natalya Osipova/Shutterstock Images, 13 (top); Volker Rauch/Shutterstock Images, 13 (bottom); lewalp/Shutterstock Images, 14 (top); Maximillian cabinet/Shutterstock Images, 14 (bottom); Sergey Uryadnikov/Shutterstock Images, 15 (top); 907Shots/Shutterstock Images, 15 (bottom); USFWS Endangered Species/Wikimedia Commons, 16 (top); Mariusz S. Jurgielewicz/Shutterstock Images, 16 (bottom); Coulanges/Shutterstock Images, 17 (bottom); Jennifer de Graaf/Shutterstock Images, 18 (top); CSNafzger/Shutterstock Images, 18 (bottom), 25 (top); Sean Lema/Shutterstock Images, 19 (top); Cavan Images/Adobe Stock Images, 19 (bottom); Down.To.Fly/Shutterstock Images, 20 (left); tab62/Shutterstock Images, 20 (right), 21 (bottom); Crissy1982/Getty Images, 22; RLS Photo/Shutterstock Images, 23 (bottom), 40 (bottom), 79, 84; Alexander Raths/Shutterstock Images, 24; Erika Kirkpatrick/Shutterstock Images, 25 (bottom); Krzysztof Winnik/Shutterstock Images, 26; Brianna Witte/Dreamstime.com, 27 (top); Hailshadow/Getty Images, 27 (bottom); Smithsonian Environmental Research Center/Wikimedia Commons, 28; JB Manning/Shutterstock Images, 29 (bottom); feathercollector/Shutterstock Images, 30 (bottom);

ABDOBOOKS.COM

Published by Abdo Reference, a division of ABDO, PO Box 398166,
Minneapolis, Minnesota 55439. Copyright © 2024 by Abdo
Consulting Group, Inc. International copyrights reserved in all
countries. No part of this book may be reproduced in any form
without written permission from the publisher. Field Guides™ is a
trademark and logo of Abdo Reference.
Printed in China

102023
012024

Editor: Leah Kaminski
Series Designer: Colleen McLaren

Library of Congress Control Number: 2023939618
Publisher's Cataloging-in-Publication Data
Names: Golkar, Golriz, author.
Title: Freshwater fish / by Golriz Golkar
Description: Minneapolis, Minnesota : Abdo Reference, 2024 |
    Series: North American field guides | Includes online resources.
Identifiers: ISBN 9781098293086 (lib. bdg.) | ISBN 9798384911029
    (ebook)
Subjects: LCSH: Freshwater fishes--Juvenile literature. | Fishes--
    Juvenile literature. | Inland water fishes--Juvenile literature. |
    Freshwater fishes--Behavior--Juvenile literature. | Encyclopedias
    and dictionaries--Juvenile literature.
Classification: DDC 597.5--dc23

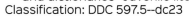